The

365 Days

to

RAISE YOUR
FREQUENCY

Journal

Melissa Alvarez

Adrema Press

Today's Date: _____*I'm Feeling:* _____

Frequency Exercise: _____

_____

_____

_____

_____

_____

_____

_____

_____

_____

My Thoughts & Results: _____

_____

_____

_____

_____

_____

_____

_____

_____

_____

_____

_____

_____

_____

Today's Date: _____*I'm Feeling:* _____

Frequency Exercise: _____

_____

_____

_____

_____

_____

_____

_____

_____

_____

_____

My Thoughts & Results: _____

_____

_____

_____

_____

_____

_____

_____

_____

_____

_____

_____

_____

_____

_____

_____

Today's Date: _____ I'm Feeling: _____

Frequency Exercise: _____

_____

_____

_____

_____

_____

_____

_____

_____

_____

_____

My Thoughts & Results: _____

_____

_____

_____

_____

_____

_____

_____

_____

_____

_____

_____

_____

_____

_____

Today's Date: _____ *I'm Feeling:* _____

Frequency Exercise: _____

_____

_____

_____

_____

_____

_____

_____

_____

_____

My Thoughts & Results: _____

_____

_____

_____

_____

_____

_____

_____

_____

_____

_____

_____

_____

_____

Today's Date: _____*I'm Feeling:* _____

Frequency Exercise: _____

_____

_____

_____

_____

_____

_____

_____

_____

_____

My Thoughts & Results: _____

_____

_____

_____

_____

_____

_____

_____

_____

_____

_____

_____

_____

_____

Today's Date: _____*I'm Feeling:* _____

Frequency Exercise: _____

_____

_____

_____

_____

_____

_____

_____

_____

_____

My Thoughts & Results: _____

_____

_____

_____

_____

_____

_____

_____

_____

_____

_____

_____

_____

_____

Today's Date: _____I'm Feeling: _____

Frequency Exercise: _____

_____

_____

_____

_____

_____

_____

_____

_____

_____

My Thoughts & Results: _____

_____

_____

_____

_____

_____

_____

_____

_____

_____

_____

_____

_____

_____

_____

Today's Date: _____ *I'm Feeling:* _____

Frequency Exercise: _____

_____

_____

_____

_____

_____

_____

_____

_____

_____

_____

My Thoughts & Results: _____

_____

_____

_____

_____

_____

_____

_____

_____

_____

_____

_____

_____

_____

_____

_____

Today's Date: _____ *I'm Feeling:* _____

Frequency Exercise: _____

_____

_____

_____

_____

_____

_____

_____

_____

_____

_____

My Thoughts & Results: _____

_____

_____

_____

_____

_____

_____

_____

_____

_____

_____

_____

_____

_____

_____

Today's Date: _____*I'm Feeling:* _____

Frequency Exercise: _____

_____

_____

_____

_____

_____

_____

_____

_____

_____

_____

My Thoughts & Results: _____

_____

_____

_____

_____

_____

_____

_____

_____

_____

_____

_____

_____

_____

_____

Today's Date: _____ *I'm Feeling:* _____

Frequency Exercise: _____

_____

_____

_____

_____

_____

_____

_____

_____

_____

_____

My Thoughts & Results: _____

_____

_____

_____

_____

_____

_____

_____

_____

_____

_____

_____

_____

_____

Today's Date: _____I'm Feeling: _____

Frequency Exercise: _____

_____
_____
_____
_____
_____
_____
_____
_____
_____
_____

My Thoughts & Results: _____

_____
_____
_____
_____
_____
_____
_____
_____
_____
_____
_____
_____
_____
_____

Today's Date: _____*I'm Feeling:* _____

Frequency Exercise: _____

_____

_____

_____

_____

_____

_____

_____

_____

_____

My Thoughts & Results: _____

_____

_____

_____

_____

_____

_____

_____

_____

_____

_____

_____

_____

_____

Today's Date: _____ I'm Feeling: _____

Frequency Exercise: _____

_____

_____

_____

_____

_____

_____

_____

_____

_____

My Thoughts & Results: _____

_____

_____

_____

_____

_____

_____

_____

_____

_____

_____

_____

_____

_____

Today's Date: _____ I'm Feeling: _____

Frequency Exercise: _____

_____

_____

_____

_____

_____

_____

_____

_____

_____

_____

My Thoughts & Results: _____

_____

_____

_____

_____

_____

_____

_____

_____

_____

_____

_____

_____

_____

_____

Today's Date: _____*I'm Feeling:* _____

Frequency Exercise: _____

_____

_____

_____

_____

_____

_____

_____

_____

_____

My Thoughts & Results: _____

_____

_____

_____

_____

_____

_____

_____

_____

_____

_____

_____

_____

_____

Today's Date: _____ *I'm Feeling:* _____

Frequency Exercise: _____

_____

_____

_____

_____

_____

_____

_____

_____

_____

My Thoughts & Results: _____

_____

_____

_____

_____

_____

_____

_____

_____

_____

_____

_____

_____

_____

Today's Date: _____ *I'm Feeling:* _____

Frequency Exercise: _____

_____

_____

_____

_____

_____

_____

_____

_____

_____

My Thoughts & Results: _____

_____

_____

_____

_____

_____

_____

_____

_____

_____

_____

_____

_____

_____

Today's Date: _____ I'm Feeling: _____

Frequency Exercise: _____

_____

_____

_____

_____

_____

_____

_____

_____

_____

My Thoughts & Results: _____

_____

_____

_____

_____

_____

_____

_____

_____

_____

_____

_____

_____

_____

Today's Date: _____ *I'm Feeling:* _____

Frequency Exercise: _____

_____

_____

_____

_____

_____

_____

_____

_____

_____

My Thoughts & Results: _____

_____

_____

_____

_____

_____

_____

_____

_____

_____

_____

_____

_____

_____

_____

Today's Date: _____ *I'm Feeling:* _____

Frequency Exercise: _____

_____

_____

_____

_____

_____

_____

_____

_____

_____

My Thoughts & Results: _____

_____

_____

_____

_____

_____

_____

_____

_____

_____

_____

_____

_____

_____

_____

Today's Date: _____ *I'm Feeling:* _____

Frequency Exercise: _____

_____

_____

_____

_____

_____

_____

_____

_____

_____

My Thoughts & Results: _____

_____

_____

_____

_____

_____

_____

_____

_____

_____

_____

_____

_____

_____

_____

Today's Date: _____I'm Feeling: _____

Frequency Exercise: _____

_____

_____

_____

_____

_____

_____

_____

_____

_____

_____

My Thoughts & Results: _____

_____

_____

_____

_____

_____

_____

_____

_____

_____

_____

_____

_____

_____

_____

Today's Date: _____I'm Feeling: _____

Frequency Exercise: _____

_____

_____

_____

_____

_____

_____

_____

_____

_____

My Thoughts & Results: _____

_____

_____

_____

_____

_____

_____

_____

_____

_____

_____

_____

_____

_____

Today's Date: _____ *I'm Feeling:* _____

Frequency Exercise: _____

_____

_____

_____

_____

_____

_____

_____

_____

_____

My Thoughts & Results: _____

_____

_____

_____

_____

_____

_____

_____

_____

_____

_____

_____

_____

_____

Today's Date: _____ *I'm Feeling:* _____

Frequency Exercise: _____

_____

_____

_____

_____

_____

_____

_____

_____

_____

My Thoughts & Results: _____

_____

_____

_____

_____

_____

_____

_____

_____

_____

_____

_____

_____

_____

Today's Date: _____*I'm Feeling:* _____

Frequency Exercise: _____

_____

_____

_____

_____

_____

_____

_____

_____

_____

My Thoughts & Results: _____

_____

_____

_____

_____

_____

_____

_____

_____

_____

_____

_____

_____

_____

Today's Date: _____*I'm Feeling:* _____

Frequency Exercise: _____

_____

_____

_____

_____

_____

_____

_____

_____

_____

_____

My Thoughts & Results: _____

_____

_____

_____

_____

_____

_____

_____

_____

_____

_____

_____

_____

_____

_____

Today's Date: _____ *I'm Feeling:* _____

Frequency Exercise: _____

_____

_____

_____

_____

_____

_____

_____

_____

_____

My Thoughts & Results: _____

_____

_____

_____

_____

_____

_____

_____

_____

_____

_____

_____

_____

_____

Today's Date: _____ *I'm Feeling:* _____

Frequency Exercise: _____

_____

_____

_____

_____

_____

_____

_____

_____

_____

My Thoughts & Results: _____

_____

_____

_____

_____

_____

_____

_____

_____

_____

_____

_____

_____

_____

Today's Date: _____ *I'm Feeling:* _____

Frequency Exercise: _____

_____

_____

_____

_____

_____

_____

_____

_____

_____

My Thoughts & Results: _____

_____

_____

_____

_____

_____

_____

_____

_____

_____

_____

_____

_____

_____

_____

Today's Date: _____*I'm Feeling:* _____

Frequency Exercise: _____

_____

_____

_____

_____

_____

_____

_____

_____

_____

My Thoughts & Results: _____

_____

_____

_____

_____

_____

_____

_____

_____

_____

_____

_____

_____

_____

Today's Date: _____ I'm Feeling: _____

Frequency Exercise: _____

_____

_____

_____

_____

_____

_____

_____

_____

_____

My Thoughts & Results: _____

_____

_____

_____

_____

_____

_____

_____

_____

_____

_____

_____

_____

_____

Today's Date: _____ I'm Feeling: _____

Frequency Exercise: _____

_____

_____

_____

_____

_____

_____

_____

_____

_____

My Thoughts & Results: _____

_____

_____

_____

_____

_____

_____

_____

_____

_____

_____

_____

_____

_____

Today's Date: _____*I'm Feeling:* _____

Frequency Exercise: _____

_____

_____

_____

_____

_____

_____

_____

_____

_____

My Thoughts & Results: _____

_____

_____

_____

_____

_____

_____

_____

_____

_____

_____

_____

_____

_____

Today's Date: _____*I'm Feeling:* _____

Frequency Exercise: _____

_____

_____

_____

_____

_____

_____

_____

_____

_____

My Thoughts & Results: _____

_____

_____

_____

_____

_____

_____

_____

_____

_____

_____

_____

_____

_____

_____

Today's Date: _____ *I'm Feeling:* _____

Frequency Exercise: _____

_____

_____

_____

_____

_____

_____

_____

_____

_____

My Thoughts & Results: _____

_____

_____

_____

_____

_____

_____

_____

_____

_____

_____

_____

_____

Today's Date: _____ I'm Feeling: _____

Frequency Exercise: _____

_____

_____

_____

_____

_____

_____

_____

_____

_____

_____

My Thoughts & Results: _____

_____

_____

_____

_____

_____

_____

_____

_____

_____

_____

_____

_____

_____

_____

Today's Date: _____*I'm Feeling:* _____

Frequency Exercise: _____

_____

_____

_____

_____

_____

_____

_____

_____

_____

My Thoughts & Results: _____

_____

_____

_____

_____

_____

_____

_____

_____

_____

_____

_____

_____

_____

Today's Date: _____ *I'm Feeling:* _____

Frequency Exercise: _____

_____

_____

_____

_____

_____

_____

_____

_____

_____

My Thoughts & Results: _____

_____

_____

_____

_____

_____

_____

_____

_____

_____

_____

_____

_____

_____

Today's Date: _____ *I'm Feeling:* _____

Frequency Exercise: _____

_____

_____

_____

_____

_____

_____

_____

_____

_____

My Thoughts & Results: _____

_____

_____

_____

_____

_____

_____

_____

_____

_____

_____

_____

_____

_____

Today's Date: _____*I'm Feeling:* _____

Frequency Exercise: _____

_____

_____

_____

_____

_____

_____

_____

_____

_____

My Thoughts & Results: _____

_____

_____

_____

_____

_____

_____

_____

_____

_____

_____

_____

_____

_____

Today's Date: _____ *I'm Feeling:* _____

Frequency Exercise: _____

_____

_____

_____

_____

_____

_____

_____

_____

_____

My Thoughts & Results: _____

_____

_____

_____

_____

_____

_____

_____

_____

_____

_____

_____

_____

_____

Today's Date: _____ *I'm Feeling:* _____

Frequency Exercise: _____

_____

_____

_____

_____

_____

_____

_____

_____

_____

_____

My Thoughts & Results: _____

_____

_____

_____

_____

_____

_____

_____

_____

_____

_____

_____

_____

_____

_____

_____

Today's Date: _____ *I'm Feeling:* _____

Frequency Exercise: _____

_____

_____

_____

_____

_____

_____

_____

_____

_____

_____

My Thoughts & Results: _____

_____

_____

_____

_____

_____

_____

_____

_____

_____

_____

_____

_____

_____

Today's Date: _____*I'm Feeling:* _____

Frequency Exercise: _____

_____

_____

_____

_____

_____

_____

_____

_____

_____

My Thoughts & Results: _____

_____

_____

_____

_____

_____

_____

_____

_____

_____

_____

_____

_____

_____

Today's Date: _____ I'm Feeling: _____

Frequency Exercise: _____

_____

_____

_____

_____

_____

_____

_____

_____

_____

My Thoughts & Results: _____

_____

_____

_____

_____

_____

_____

_____

_____

_____

_____

_____

_____

_____

Today's Date: _____ *I'm Feeling:* _____

Frequency Exercise: _____

_____

_____

_____

_____

_____

_____

_____

_____

_____

My Thoughts & Results: _____

_____

_____

_____

_____

_____

_____

_____

_____

_____

_____

_____

_____

_____

_____

Today's Date: _____ *I'm Feeling:* _____

Frequency Exercise: _____

_____

_____

_____

_____

_____

_____

_____

_____

_____

My Thoughts & Results: _____

_____

_____

_____

_____

_____

_____

_____

_____

_____

_____

_____

_____

Today's Date: _____ *I'm Feeling:* _____

Frequency Exercise: _____

_____

_____

_____

_____

_____

_____

_____

_____

_____

_____

My Thoughts & Results: _____

_____

_____

_____

_____

_____

_____

_____

_____

_____

_____

_____

_____

_____

_____

Today's Date: _____I'm Feeling: _____

Frequency Exercise: _____

_____

_____

_____

_____

_____

_____

_____

_____

_____

My Thoughts & Results: _____

_____

_____

_____

_____

_____

_____

_____

_____

_____

_____

_____

_____

_____

Today's Date: _____ *I'm Feeling:* _____

Frequency Exercise: _____

_____

_____

_____

_____

_____

_____

_____

_____

_____

_____

My Thoughts & Results: _____

_____

_____

_____

_____

_____

_____

_____

_____

_____

_____

_____

_____

_____

_____

Today's Date: _____ *I'm Feeling:* _____

Frequency Exercise: _____

_____

_____

_____

_____

_____

_____

_____

_____

_____

My Thoughts & Results: _____

_____

_____

_____

_____

_____

_____

_____

_____

_____

_____

_____

_____

_____

_____

Today's Date: _____*I'm Feeling:* _____

Frequency Exercise: _____

_____

_____

_____

_____

_____

_____

_____

_____

_____

My Thoughts & Results: _____

_____

_____

_____

_____

_____

_____

_____

_____

_____

_____

_____

_____

_____

Today's Date: _____ *I'm Feeling:* _____

Frequency Exercise: _____

_____

_____

_____

_____

_____

_____

_____

_____

_____

My Thoughts & Results: _____

_____

_____

_____

_____

_____

_____

_____

_____

_____

_____

_____

_____

_____

Today's Date: _____*I'm Feeling:* _____

Frequency Exercise: _____

_____

_____

_____

_____

_____

_____

_____

_____

_____

_____

My Thoughts & Results: _____

_____

_____

_____

_____

_____

_____

_____

_____

_____

_____

_____

_____

_____

_____

_____

Today's Date: _____I'm Feeling: _____

Frequency Exercise: _____

_____

_____

_____

_____

_____

_____

_____

_____

_____

_____

My Thoughts & Results: _____

_____

_____

_____

_____

_____

_____

_____

_____

_____

_____

_____

_____

_____

Today's Date: _____ *I'm Feeling:* _____

Frequency Exercise: _____

_____

_____

_____

_____

_____

_____

_____

_____

_____

My Thoughts & Results: _____

_____

_____

_____

_____

_____

_____

_____

_____

_____

_____

_____

_____

_____

_____

Today's Date: _____I'm Feeling: _____

Frequency Exercise: _____

_____

_____

_____

_____

_____

_____

_____

_____

_____

My Thoughts & Results: _____

_____

_____

_____

_____

_____

_____

_____

_____

_____

_____

_____

_____

Today's Date: _____*I'm Feeling:* _____

Frequency Exercise: _____

_____

_____

_____

_____

_____

_____

_____

_____

_____

My Thoughts & Results: _____

_____

_____

_____

_____

_____

_____

_____

_____

_____

_____

_____

_____

_____

Today's Date: _____*I'm Feeling:* _____

Frequency Exercise: _____

_____

_____

_____

_____

_____

_____

_____

_____

_____

My Thoughts & Results: _____

_____

_____

_____

_____

_____

_____

_____

_____

_____

_____

_____

_____

_____

Today's Date: _____ *I'm Feeling:* _____

Frequency Exercise: _____

_____

_____

_____

_____

_____

_____

_____

_____

_____

My Thoughts & Results: _____

_____

_____

_____

_____

_____

_____

_____

_____

_____

_____

_____

_____

_____

Today's Date: _____ I'm Feeling: _____

Frequency Exercise: _____

_____

_____

_____

_____

_____

_____

_____

_____

_____

My Thoughts & Results: _____

_____

_____

_____

_____

_____

_____

_____

_____

_____

_____

_____

_____

_____

Today's Date: _____ *I'm Feeling:* _____

Frequency Exercise: _____

_____

_____

_____

_____

_____

_____

_____

_____

_____

My Thoughts & Results: _____

_____

_____

_____

_____

_____

_____

_____

_____

_____

_____

_____

_____

_____

Today's Date: _____ *I'm Feeling:* _____

Frequency Exercise: _____

_____

_____

_____

_____

_____

_____

_____

_____

_____

My Thoughts & Results: _____

_____

_____

_____

_____

_____

_____

_____

_____

_____

_____

_____

_____

_____

Today's Date: _____ *I'm Feeling:* _____

Frequency Exercise: _____

_____

_____

_____

_____

_____

_____

_____

_____

_____

My Thoughts & Results: _____

_____

_____

_____

_____

_____

_____

_____

_____

_____

_____

_____

_____

_____

Today's Date: _____I'm Feeling: _____

Frequency Exercise: _____

_____

_____

_____

_____

_____

_____

_____

_____

_____

_____

My Thoughts & Results: _____

_____

_____

_____

_____

_____

_____

_____

_____

_____

_____

_____

_____

_____

Today's Date: _____I'm Feeling: _____

Frequency Exercise: _____

_____

_____

_____

_____

_____

_____

_____

_____

_____

_____

My Thoughts & Results: _____

_____

_____

_____

_____

_____

_____

_____

_____

_____

_____

_____

_____

_____

Today's Date: _____ *I'm Feeling:* _____

Frequency Exercise: _____

_____

_____

_____

_____

_____

_____

_____

_____

_____

My Thoughts & Results: _____

_____

_____

_____

_____

_____

_____

_____

_____

_____

_____

_____

_____

Today's Date: _____ I'm Feeling: _____

Frequency Exercise: _____

_____

_____

_____

_____

_____

_____

_____

_____

_____

My Thoughts & Results: _____

_____

_____

_____

_____

_____

_____

_____

_____

_____

_____

_____

_____

_____

Today's Date: _____I'm Feeling: _____

Frequency Exercise: _____

_____

_____

_____

_____

_____

_____

_____

_____

_____

My Thoughts & Results: _____

_____

_____

_____

_____

_____

_____

_____

_____

_____

_____

_____

_____

Today's Date: _____I'm Feeling: _____

Frequency Exercise: _____

_____

_____

_____

_____

_____

_____

_____

_____

_____

My Thoughts & Results: _____

_____

_____

_____

_____

_____

_____

_____

_____

_____

_____

_____

_____

_____

Today's Date: _____ I'm Feeling: _____

Frequency Exercise: _____

_____

_____

_____

_____

_____

_____

_____

_____

_____

My Thoughts & Results: _____

_____

_____

_____

_____

_____

_____

_____

_____

_____

_____

_____

_____

_____

Today's Date: _____I'm Feeling: _____

Frequency Exercise: _____

_____

_____

_____

_____

_____

_____

_____

_____

_____

My Thoughts & Results: _____

_____

_____

_____

_____

_____

_____

_____

_____

_____

_____

_____

_____

_____

_____

Today's Date: _____ *I'm Feeling:* _____

Frequency Exercise: _____

_____

_____

_____

_____

_____

_____

_____

_____

_____

My Thoughts & Results: _____

_____

_____

_____

_____

_____

_____

_____

_____

_____

_____

_____

_____

_____

Today's Date: _____*I'm Feeling:* _____

Frequency Exercise: _____

_____

_____

_____

_____

_____

_____

_____

_____

_____

My Thoughts & Results: _____

_____

_____

_____

_____

_____

_____

_____

_____

_____

_____

_____

_____

Today's Date: _____ *I'm Feeling:* _____

Frequency Exercise: _____

_____

_____

_____

_____

_____

_____

_____

_____

_____

My Thoughts & Results: _____

_____

_____

_____

_____

_____

_____

_____

_____

_____

_____

_____

_____

_____

Today's Date: _____ *I'm Feeling:* _____

Frequency Exercise: _____

_____

_____

_____

_____

_____

_____

_____

_____

_____

_____

My Thoughts & Results: _____

_____

_____

_____

_____

_____

_____

_____

_____

_____

_____

_____

_____

_____

Today's Date: _____ I'm Feeling: _____

Frequency Exercise: _____

_____

_____

_____

_____

_____

_____

_____

_____

_____

My Thoughts & Results: _____

_____

_____

_____

_____

_____

_____

_____

_____

_____

_____

_____

_____

Today's Date: _____ *I'm Feeling:* _____

Frequency Exercise: _____

_____

_____

_____

_____

_____

_____

_____

_____

_____

My Thoughts & Results: _____

_____

_____

_____

_____

_____

_____

_____

_____

_____

_____

_____

_____

_____

_____

Today's Date: _____I'm Feeling: _____

Frequency Exercise: _____

_____

_____

_____

_____

_____

_____

_____

_____

_____

My Thoughts & Results: _____

_____

_____

_____

_____

_____

_____

_____

_____

_____

_____

_____

_____

Today's Date: _____*I'm Feeling:* _____

Frequency Exercise: _____

_____

_____

_____

_____

_____

_____

_____

_____

_____

My Thoughts & Results: _____

_____

_____

_____

_____

_____

_____

_____

_____

_____

_____

_____

_____

_____

Today's Date: _____ I'm Feeling: _____

Frequency Exercise: _____

_____

_____

_____

_____

_____

_____

_____

_____

_____

_____

My Thoughts & Results: _____

_____

_____

_____

_____

_____

_____

_____

_____

_____

_____

_____

_____

_____

Today's Date: _____*I'm Feeling:* _____

Frequency Exercise: _____

_____

_____

_____

_____

_____

_____

_____

_____

_____

My Thoughts & Results: _____

_____

_____

_____

_____

_____

_____

_____

_____

_____

_____

_____

_____

_____

Today's Date: _____*I'm Feeling:* _____

Frequency Exercise: _____

_____

_____

_____

_____

_____

_____

_____

_____

_____

My Thoughts & Results: _____

_____

_____

_____

_____

_____

_____

_____

_____

_____

_____

_____

_____

_____

Today's Date: _____ *I'm Feeling:* _____

Frequency Exercise: _____

_____

_____

_____

_____

_____

_____

_____

_____

_____

My Thoughts & Results: _____

_____

_____

_____

_____

_____

_____

_____

_____

_____

_____

_____

_____

_____

Today's Date: _____*I'm Feeling:* _____

Frequency Exercise: _____

_____

_____

_____

_____

_____

_____

_____

_____

_____

My Thoughts & Results: _____

_____

_____

_____

_____

_____

_____

_____

_____

_____

_____

_____

_____

Today's Date: _____*I'm Feeling:* _____

Frequency Exercise: _____

_____

_____

_____

_____

_____

_____

_____

_____

_____

My Thoughts & Results: _____

_____

_____

_____

_____

_____

_____

_____

_____

_____

_____

_____

_____

_____

Today's Date: _____ I'm Feeling: _____

Frequency Exercise: _____

_____

_____

_____

_____

_____

_____

_____

_____

_____

My Thoughts & Results: _____

_____

_____

_____

_____

_____

_____

_____

_____

_____

_____

_____

_____

Today's Date: _____ *I'm Feeling:* _____

Frequency Exercise: _____

_____

_____

_____

_____

_____

_____

_____

_____

_____

My Thoughts & Results: _____

_____

_____

_____

_____

_____

_____

_____

_____

_____

_____

_____

_____

_____

Today's Date: _____ *I'm Feeling:* _____

Frequency Exercise: _____

_____

_____

_____

_____

_____

_____

_____

_____

_____

My Thoughts & Results: _____

_____

_____

_____

_____

_____

_____

_____

_____

_____

_____

_____

_____

_____

_____

Today's Date: _____ I'm Feeling: _____

Frequency Exercise: _____

_____

_____

_____

_____

_____

_____

_____

_____

_____

My Thoughts & Results: _____

_____

_____

_____

_____

_____

_____

_____

_____

_____

_____

_____

_____

_____

Today's Date: _____I'm Feeling: _____

Frequency Exercise: _____

_____

_____

_____

_____

_____

_____

_____

_____

_____

My Thoughts & Results: _____

_____

_____

_____

_____

_____

_____

_____

_____

_____

_____

_____

_____

Today's Date: _____I'm Feeling: _____

Frequency Exercise: _____

_____

_____

_____

_____

_____

_____

_____

_____

_____

My Thoughts & Results: _____

_____

_____

_____

_____

_____

_____

_____

_____

_____

_____

_____

_____

_____

Today's Date: _____ I'm Feeling: _____

Frequency Exercise: _____

_____

_____

_____

_____

_____

_____

_____

_____

_____

My Thoughts & Results: _____

_____

_____

_____

_____

_____

_____

_____

_____

_____

_____

_____

_____

Today's Date: _____ *I'm Feeling:* _____

Frequency Exercise: _____

_____

_____

_____

_____

_____

_____

_____

_____

_____

My Thoughts & Results: _____

_____

_____

_____

_____

_____

_____

_____

_____

_____

_____

_____

_____

_____

_____

Today's Date: _____ *I'm Feeling:* _____

Frequency Exercise: _____

_____

_____

_____

_____

_____

_____

_____

_____

_____

My Thoughts & Results: _____

_____

_____

_____

_____

_____

_____

_____

_____

_____

_____

_____

_____

_____

Today's Date: _____ I'm Feeling: _____

Frequency Exercise: _____

_____

_____

_____

_____

_____

_____

_____

_____

_____

My Thoughts & Results: _____

_____

_____

_____

_____

_____

_____

_____

_____

_____

_____

_____

_____

_____

_____

Today's Date: _____ *I'm Feeling:* _____

Frequency Exercise: _____

_____

_____

_____

_____

_____

_____

_____

_____

_____

My Thoughts & Results: _____

_____

_____

_____

_____

_____

_____

_____

_____

_____

_____

_____

_____

Today's Date: _____*I'm Feeling:* _____

Frequency Exercise: _____

_____

_____

_____

_____

_____

_____

_____

_____

_____

_____

My Thoughts & Results: _____

_____

_____

_____

_____

_____

_____

_____

_____

_____

_____

_____

_____

_____

_____

Today's Date: _____*I'm Feeling:* _____

Frequency Exercise: _____

_____

_____

_____

_____

_____

_____

_____

_____

_____

My Thoughts & Results: _____

_____

_____

_____

_____

_____

_____

_____

_____

_____

_____

_____

_____

_____

Today's Date: _____I'm Feeling: _____

Frequency Exercise: _____

_____

_____

_____

_____

_____

_____

_____

_____

_____

My Thoughts & Results: _____

_____

_____

_____

_____

_____

_____

_____

_____

_____

_____

_____

_____

_____

Today's Date: _____ *I'm Feeling:* _____

Frequency Exercise: _____

_____

_____

_____

_____

_____

_____

_____

_____

_____

My Thoughts & Results: _____

_____

_____

_____

_____

_____

_____

_____

_____

_____

_____

_____

_____

_____

Today's Date: _____ I'm Feeling: _____

Frequency Exercise: _____

_____

_____

_____

_____

_____

_____

_____

_____

_____

My Thoughts & Results: _____

_____

_____

_____

_____

_____

_____

_____

_____

_____

_____

_____

_____

_____

_____

Today's Date: _____ I'm Feeling: _____

Frequency Exercise: _____

_____

_____

_____

_____

_____

_____

_____

_____

_____

My Thoughts & Results: _____

_____

_____

_____

_____

_____

_____

_____

_____

_____

_____

_____

_____

Today's Date: _____ *I'm Feeling:* _____

Frequency Exercise: _____

_____

_____

_____

_____

_____

_____

_____

_____

_____

_____

My Thoughts & Results: _____

_____

_____

_____

_____

_____

_____

_____

_____

_____

_____

_____

_____

_____

_____

Today's Date: _____ I'm Feeling: _____

Frequency Exercise: _____

_____

_____

_____

_____

_____

_____

_____

_____

_____

_____

My Thoughts & Results: _____

_____

_____

_____

_____

_____

_____

_____

_____

_____

_____

_____

_____

_____

Today's Date: _____*I'm Feeling:* _____

Frequency Exercise: _____

_____

_____

_____

_____

_____

_____

_____

_____

_____

My Thoughts & Results: _____

_____

_____

_____

_____

_____

_____

_____

_____

_____

_____

_____

_____

_____

Today's Date: _____ *I'm Feeling:* _____

Frequency Exercise: _____

_____

_____

_____

_____

_____

_____

_____

_____

_____

My Thoughts & Results: _____

_____

_____

_____

_____

_____

_____

_____

_____

_____

_____

_____

_____

_____

Today's Date: _____ *I'm Feeling:* _____

Frequency Exercise: _____

_____

_____

_____

_____

_____

_____

_____

_____

_____

My Thoughts & Results: _____

_____

_____

_____

_____

_____

_____

_____

_____

_____

_____

_____

_____

_____

Today's Date: _____*I'm Feeling:* _____

Frequency Exercise: _____

_____

_____

_____

_____

_____

_____

_____

_____

_____

My Thoughts & Results: _____

_____

_____

_____

_____

_____

_____

_____

_____

_____

_____

_____

_____

Today's Date: _____*I'm Feeling:* _____

Frequency Exercise: _____

_____

_____

_____

_____

_____

_____

_____

_____

_____

_____

My Thoughts & Results: _____

_____

_____

_____

_____

_____

_____

_____

_____

_____

_____

_____

_____

_____

Today's Date: _____ I'm Feeling: _____

Frequency Exercise: _____

_____

_____

_____

_____

_____

_____

_____

_____

_____

My Thoughts & Results: _____

_____

_____

_____

_____

_____

_____

_____

_____

_____

_____

_____

_____

_____

Today's Date: _____ I'm Feeling: _____

Frequency Exercise: _____

_____

_____

_____

_____

_____

_____

_____

_____

_____

My Thoughts & Results: _____

_____

_____

_____

_____

_____

_____

_____

_____

_____

_____

_____

_____

Today's Date: _____ *I'm Feeling:* _____

Frequency Exercise: _____

_____

_____

_____

_____

_____

_____

_____

_____

_____

My Thoughts & Results: _____

_____

_____

_____

_____

_____

_____

_____

_____

_____

_____

_____

_____

_____

Today's Date: _____ *I'm Feeling:* _____

Frequency Exercise: _____

_____

_____

_____

_____

_____

_____

_____

_____

_____

My Thoughts & Results: _____

_____

_____

_____

_____

_____

_____

_____

_____

_____

_____

_____

_____

_____

Today's Date: _____I'm Feeling: _____

Frequency Exercise: _____

_____

_____

_____

_____

_____

_____

_____

_____

_____

My Thoughts & Results: _____

_____

_____

_____

_____

_____

_____

_____

_____

_____

_____

_____

_____

Today's Date: _____ I'm Feeling: _____

Frequency Exercise: _____

_____

_____

_____

_____

_____

_____

_____

_____

_____

My Thoughts & Results: _____

_____

_____

_____

_____

_____

_____

_____

_____

_____

_____

_____

_____

_____

Today's Date: _____ I'm Feeling: _____

Frequency Exercise: _____

_____

_____

_____

_____

_____

_____

_____

_____

_____

My Thoughts & Results: _____

_____

_____

_____

_____

_____

_____

_____

_____

_____

_____

_____

_____

_____

Today's Date: _____*I'm Feeling:* _____

Frequency Exercise: _____

_____

_____

_____

_____

_____

_____

_____

_____

_____

_____

My Thoughts & Results: _____

_____

_____

_____

_____

_____

_____

_____

_____

_____

_____

_____

_____

_____

_____

Today's Date: _____ *I'm Feeling:* _____

Frequency Exercise: _____

_____

_____

_____

_____

_____

_____

_____

_____

_____

My Thoughts & Results: _____

_____

_____

_____

_____

_____

_____

_____

_____

_____

_____

_____

_____

_____

Today's Date: _____ I'm Feeling: _____

Frequency Exercise: _____

_____

_____

_____

_____

_____

_____

_____

_____

_____

My Thoughts & Results: _____

_____

_____

_____

_____

_____

_____

_____

_____

_____

_____

_____

_____

_____

Today's Date: _____*I'm Feeling:* _____

Frequency Exercise: _____

_____

_____

_____

_____

_____

_____

_____

_____

_____

My Thoughts & Results: _____

_____

_____

_____

_____

_____

_____

_____

_____

_____

_____

_____

_____

_____

Today's Date: _____ *I'm Feeling:* _____

Frequency Exercise: _____

_____

_____

_____

_____

_____

_____

_____

_____

_____

_____

My Thoughts & Results: _____

_____

_____

_____

_____

_____

_____

_____

_____

_____

_____

_____

_____

_____

Today's Date: _____ I'm Feeling: _____

Frequency Exercise: _____

_____

_____

_____

_____

_____

_____

_____

_____

_____

My Thoughts & Results: _____

_____

_____

_____

_____

_____

_____

_____

_____

_____

_____

_____

_____

Today's Date: _____ *I'm Feeling:* _____

Frequency Exercise: _____

_____

_____

_____

_____

_____

_____

_____

_____

_____

_____

My Thoughts & Results: _____

_____

_____

_____

_____

_____

_____

_____

_____

_____

_____

_____

_____

_____

_____

Today's Date: _____ I'm Feeling: _____

Frequency Exercise: _____

_____

_____

_____

_____

_____

_____

_____

_____

_____

My Thoughts & Results: _____

_____

_____

_____

_____

_____

_____

_____

_____

_____

_____

_____

_____

Today's Date: _____ *I'm Feeling:* _____

Frequency Exercise: _____

_____

_____

_____

_____

_____

_____

_____

_____

_____

_____

My Thoughts & Results: _____

_____

_____

_____

_____

_____

_____

_____

_____

_____

_____

_____

_____

_____

_____

Today's Date: _____ *I'm Feeling:* _____

Frequency Exercise: _____

_____

_____

_____

_____

_____

_____

_____

_____

_____

_____

My Thoughts & Results: _____

_____

_____

_____

_____

_____

_____

_____

_____

_____

_____

_____

_____

_____

Today's Date: _____ *I'm Feeling:* _____

Frequency Exercise: _____

_____

_____

_____

_____

_____

_____

_____

_____

_____

My Thoughts & Results: _____

_____

_____

_____

_____

_____

_____

_____

_____

_____

_____

_____

_____

Today's Date: _____*I'm Feeling:* _____

Frequency Exercise: _____

_____

_____

_____

_____

_____

_____

_____

_____

_____

My Thoughts & Results: _____

_____

_____

_____

_____

_____

_____

_____

_____

_____

_____

_____

_____

Today's Date: _____ *I'm Feeling:* _____

Frequency Exercise: _____

_____

_____

_____

_____

_____

_____

_____

_____

_____

My Thoughts & Results: _____

_____

_____

_____

_____

_____

_____

_____

_____

_____

_____

_____

_____

_____

Today's Date: _____ I'm Feeling: _____

Frequency Exercise: _____

_____

_____

_____

_____

_____

_____

_____

_____

_____

My Thoughts & Results: _____

_____

_____

_____

_____

_____

_____

_____

_____

_____

_____

_____

_____

Today's Date: _____ *I'm Feeling:* _____

Frequency Exercise: _____

_____

_____

_____

_____

_____

_____

_____

_____

_____

_____

My Thoughts & Results: _____

_____

_____

_____

_____

_____

_____

_____

_____

_____

_____

_____

_____

_____

_____

Today's Date: _____I'm Feeling: _____

Frequency Exercise: _____

_____

_____

_____

_____

_____

_____

_____

_____

_____

My Thoughts & Results: _____

_____

_____

_____

_____

_____

_____

_____

_____

_____

_____

_____

_____

Today's Date: _____ *I'm Feeling:* _____

Frequency Exercise: _____

_____

_____

_____

_____

_____

_____

_____

_____

_____

My Thoughts & Results: _____

_____

_____

_____

_____

_____

_____

_____

_____

_____

_____

_____

_____

_____

Today's Date: _____ I'm Feeling: _____

Frequency Exercise: _____

_____

_____

_____

_____

_____

_____

_____

_____

_____

My Thoughts & Results: _____

_____

_____

_____

_____

_____

_____

_____

_____

_____

_____

_____

_____

_____

Today's Date: _____*I'm Feeling:* _____

Frequency Exercise: _____

_____

_____

_____

_____

_____

_____

_____

_____

_____

My Thoughts & Results: _____

_____

_____

_____

_____

_____

_____

_____

_____

_____

_____

_____

_____

_____

Today's Date: _____ *I'm Feeling:* _____

Frequency Exercise: _____

_____

_____

_____

_____

_____

_____

_____

_____

_____

My Thoughts & Results: _____

_____

_____

_____

_____

_____

_____

_____

_____

_____

_____

_____

_____

_____

Today's Date: _____ *I'm Feeling:* _____

Frequency Exercise: _____

_____

_____

_____

_____

_____

_____

_____

_____

_____

_____

My Thoughts & Results: _____

_____

_____

_____

_____

_____

_____

_____

_____

_____

_____

_____

_____

_____

_____

Today's Date: _____ *I'm Feeling:* _____

Frequency Exercise: _____

_____

_____

_____

_____

_____

_____

_____

_____

_____

My Thoughts & Results: _____

_____

_____

_____

_____

_____

_____

_____

_____

_____

_____

_____

_____

Today's Date: _____I'm Feeling: _____

Frequency Exercise: _____

_____

_____

_____

_____

_____

_____

_____

_____

_____

My Thoughts & Results: _____

_____

_____

_____

_____

_____

_____

_____

_____

_____

_____

_____

_____

Today's Date: _____ I'm Feeling: _____

Frequency Exercise: _____

_____

_____

_____

_____

_____

_____

_____

_____

_____

My Thoughts & Results: _____

_____

_____

_____

_____

_____

_____

_____

_____

_____

_____

_____

_____

_____

Today's Date: _____ *I'm Feeling:* _____

Frequency Exercise: _____

_____

_____

_____

_____

_____

_____

_____

_____

_____

My Thoughts & Results: _____

_____

_____

_____

_____

_____

_____

_____

_____

_____

_____

_____

_____

Today's Date: _____ *I'm Feeling:* _____

Frequency Exercise: _____

_____

_____

_____

_____

_____

_____

_____

_____

_____

My Thoughts & Results: _____

_____

_____

_____

_____

_____

_____

_____

_____

_____

_____

_____

_____

_____

Today's Date: _____I'm Feeling: _____

Frequency Exercise: _____

_____

_____

_____

_____

_____

_____

_____

_____

_____

My Thoughts & Results: _____

_____

_____

_____

_____

_____

_____

_____

_____

_____

_____

_____

_____

_____

Today's Date: _____ *I'm Feeling:* _____

Frequency Exercise: _____

_____

_____

_____

_____

_____

_____

_____

_____

_____

My Thoughts & Results: _____

_____

_____

_____

_____

_____

_____

_____

_____

_____

_____

_____

_____

Today's Date: _____ *I'm Feeling:* _____

Frequency Exercise: _____

_____

_____

_____

_____

_____

_____

_____

_____

_____

My Thoughts & Results: _____

_____

_____

_____

_____

_____

_____

_____

_____

_____

_____

_____

_____

_____

_____

Today's Date: _____*I'm Feeling:* _____

Frequency Exercise: _____

_____

_____

_____

_____

_____

_____

_____

_____

_____

My Thoughts & Results: _____

_____

_____

_____

_____

_____

_____

_____

_____

_____

_____

_____

_____

_____

Today's Date: _____*I'm Feeling:* _____

Frequency Exercise: _____

_____

_____

_____

_____

_____

_____

_____

_____

_____

My Thoughts & Results: _____

_____

_____

_____

_____

_____

_____

_____

_____

_____

_____

_____

_____

_____

Today's Date: _____ I'm Feeling: _____

Frequency Exercise: _____

_____

_____

_____

_____

_____

_____

_____

_____

_____

My Thoughts & Results: _____

_____

_____

_____

_____

_____

_____

_____

_____

_____

_____

_____

_____

Today's Date: _____ *I'm Feeling:* _____

Frequency Exercise: _____

_____

_____

_____

_____

_____

_____

_____

_____

_____

My Thoughts & Results: _____

_____

_____

_____

_____

_____

_____

_____

_____

_____

_____

_____

_____

_____

Today's Date: _____*I'm Feeling:* _____

Frequency Exercise: _____

_____

_____

_____

_____

_____

_____

_____

_____

_____

My Thoughts & Results: _____

_____

_____

_____

_____

_____

_____

_____

_____

_____

_____

_____

_____

_____

Today's Date: _____ I'm Feeling: _____

Frequency Exercise: _____

_____

_____

_____

_____

_____

_____

_____

_____

_____

_____

My Thoughts & Results: _____

_____

_____

_____

_____

_____

_____

_____

_____

_____

_____

_____

_____

_____

Today's Date: _____ I'm Feeling: _____

Frequency Exercise: _____

_____

_____

_____

_____

_____

_____

_____

_____

My Thoughts & Results: _____

_____

_____

_____

_____

_____

_____

_____

_____

_____

_____

_____

_____

Today's Date: _____I'm Feeling: _____

Frequency Exercise: _____

_____

_____

_____

_____

_____

_____

_____

_____

_____

_____

My Thoughts & Results: _____

_____

_____

_____

_____

_____

_____

_____

_____

_____

_____

_____

_____

_____

_____

Today's Date: _____*I'm Feeling:* _____

Frequency Exercise: _____

_____

_____

_____

_____

_____

_____

_____

_____

_____

My Thoughts & Results: _____

_____

_____

_____

_____

_____

_____

_____

_____

_____

_____

_____

_____

Today's Date: _____ I'm Feeling: _____

Frequency Exercise: _____

_____

_____

_____

_____

_____

_____

_____

_____

_____

My Thoughts & Results: _____

_____

_____

_____

_____

_____

_____

_____

_____

_____

_____

_____

_____

_____

_____

Today's Date: _____ *I'm Feeling:* _____

Frequency Exercise: _____

_____

_____

_____

_____

_____

_____

_____

_____

_____

My Thoughts & Results: _____

_____

_____

_____

_____

_____

_____

_____

_____

_____

_____

_____

_____

Today's Date: _____*I'm Feeling:* _____

Frequency Exercise: _____

_____

_____

_____

_____

_____

_____

_____

_____

_____

My Thoughts & Results: _____

_____

_____

_____

_____

_____

_____

_____

_____

_____

_____

_____

_____

_____

Today's Date: _____ *I'm Feeling:* _____

Frequency Exercise: _____

_____

_____

_____

_____

_____

_____

_____

_____

_____

My Thoughts & Results: _____

_____

_____

_____

_____

_____

_____

_____

_____

_____

_____

_____

_____

Today's Date: _____I'm Feeling: _____

Frequency Exercise: _____

_____

_____

_____

_____

_____

_____

_____

_____

_____

My Thoughts & Results: _____

_____

_____

_____

_____

_____

_____

_____

_____

_____

_____

_____

_____

_____

Today's Date: _____ *I'm Feeling:* _____

Frequency Exercise: _____

_____

_____

_____

_____

_____

_____

_____

_____

_____

My Thoughts & Results: _____

_____

_____

_____

_____

_____

_____

_____

_____

_____

_____

_____

_____

_____

Today's Date: _____ *I'm Feeling:* _____

Frequency Exercise: _____

_____

_____

_____

_____

_____

_____

_____

_____

_____

My Thoughts & Results: _____

_____

_____

_____

_____

_____

_____

_____

_____

_____

_____

_____

_____

Today's Date: _____ *I'm Feeling:* _____

Frequency Exercise: _____

_____

_____

_____

_____

_____

_____

_____

_____

_____

My Thoughts & Results: _____

_____

_____

_____

_____

_____

_____

_____

_____

_____

_____

_____

_____

Today's Date: _____*I'm Feeling:* _____

Frequency Exercise: _____

_____

_____

_____

_____

_____

_____

_____

_____

_____

_____

My Thoughts & Results: _____

_____

_____

_____

_____

_____

_____

_____

_____

_____

_____

_____

_____

_____

Today's Date: _____ I'm Feeling: _____

Frequency Exercise: _____

_____

_____

_____

_____

_____

_____

_____

_____

_____

My Thoughts & Results: _____

_____

_____

_____

_____

_____

_____

_____

_____

_____

_____

_____

_____

_____

Today's Date: _____ I'm Feeling: _____

Frequency Exercise: _____

_____

_____

_____

_____

_____

_____

_____

_____

_____

My Thoughts & Results: _____

_____

_____

_____

_____

_____

_____

_____

_____

_____

_____

_____

_____

_____

Today's Date: _____ *I'm Feeling:* _____

Frequency Exercise: _____

_____

_____

_____

_____

_____

_____

_____

_____

_____

My Thoughts & Results: _____

_____

_____

_____

_____

_____

_____

_____

_____

_____

_____

_____

_____

_____

Today's Date: _____ *I'm Feeling:* _____

Frequency Exercise: _____

_____

_____

_____

_____

_____

_____

_____

_____

_____

My Thoughts & Results: _____

_____

_____

_____

_____

_____

_____

_____

_____

_____

_____

_____

_____

_____

_____

Today's Date: _____*I'm Feeling:* _____

Frequency Exercise: _____

_____

_____

_____

_____

_____

_____

_____

_____

_____

My Thoughts & Results: _____

_____

_____

_____

_____

_____

_____

_____

_____

_____

_____

_____

_____

_____

Today's Date: _____*I'm Feeling:* _____

Frequency Exercise: _____

_____

_____

_____

_____

_____

_____

_____

_____

_____

_____

My Thoughts & Results: _____

_____

_____

_____

_____

_____

_____

_____

_____

_____

_____

_____

_____

_____

_____

Today's Date: _____I'm Feeling: _____

Frequency Exercise: _____

_____

_____

_____

_____

_____

_____

_____

_____

_____

My Thoughts & Results: _____

_____

_____

_____

_____

_____

_____

_____

_____

_____

_____

_____

_____

Today's Date: _____ *I'm Feeling:* _____

Frequency Exercise: _____

_____

_____

_____

_____

_____

_____

_____

_____

_____

My Thoughts & Results: _____

_____

_____

_____

_____

_____

_____

_____

_____

_____

_____

_____

_____

Today's Date: _____I'm Feeling: _____

Frequency Exercise: _____

_____

_____

_____

_____

_____

_____

_____

_____

_____

My Thoughts & Results: _____

_____

_____

_____

_____

_____

_____

_____

_____

_____

_____

_____

_____

_____

Today's Date: _____ *I'm Feeling:* _____

Frequency Exercise: _____

_____

_____

_____

_____

_____

_____

_____

_____

_____

My Thoughts & Results: _____

_____

_____

_____

_____

_____

_____

_____

_____

_____

_____

_____

_____

_____

Today's Date: _____*I'm Feeling:* _____

Frequency Exercise: _____

_____

_____

_____

_____

_____

_____

_____

_____

_____

My Thoughts & Results: _____

_____

_____

_____

_____

_____

_____

_____

_____

_____

_____

_____

_____

_____

Today's Date: _____ *I'm Feeling:* _____

Frequency Exercise: _____

_____

_____

_____

_____

_____

_____

_____

_____

_____

My Thoughts & Results: _____

_____

_____

_____

_____

_____

_____

_____

_____

_____

_____

_____

_____

_____

Today's Date: _____*I'm Feeling:* _____

Frequency Exercise: _____

_____

_____

_____

_____

_____

_____

_____

_____

_____

My Thoughts & Results: _____

_____

_____

_____

_____

_____

_____

_____

_____

_____

_____

_____

_____

_____

Today's Date: _____I'm Feeling: _____

Frequency Exercise: _____

_____

_____

_____

_____

_____

_____

_____

_____

_____

My Thoughts & Results: _____

_____

_____

_____

_____

_____

_____

_____

_____

_____

_____

_____

_____

_____

Today's Date: _____*I'm Feeling:* _____

Frequency Exercise: _____

_____

_____

_____

_____

_____

_____

_____

_____

_____

My Thoughts & Results: _____

_____

_____

_____

_____

_____

_____

_____

_____

_____

_____

_____

_____

Today's Date: _____ *I'm Feeling:* _____

Frequency Exercise: _____

_____

_____

_____

_____

_____

_____

_____

_____

_____

_____

My Thoughts & Results: _____

_____

_____

_____

_____

_____

_____

_____

_____

_____

_____

_____

_____

_____

_____

Today's Date: _____ *I'm Feeling:* _____

Frequency Exercise: _____

_____

_____

_____

_____

_____

_____

_____

_____

_____

My Thoughts & Results: _____

_____

_____

_____

_____

_____

_____

_____

_____

_____

_____

_____

_____

_____

Today's Date: _____ *I'm Feeling:* _____

Frequency Exercise: _____

_____

_____

_____

_____

_____

_____

_____

_____

_____

My Thoughts & Results: _____

_____

_____

_____

_____

_____

_____

_____

_____

_____

_____

_____

_____

_____

Today's Date: _____ *I'm Feeling:* _____

Frequency Exercise: _____

_____

_____

_____

_____

_____

_____

_____

_____

_____

My Thoughts & Results: _____

_____

_____

_____

_____

_____

_____

_____

_____

_____

_____

_____

_____

_____

Today's Date: _____ I'm Feeling: _____

Frequency Exercise: _____

_____

_____

_____

_____

_____

_____

_____

_____

_____

_____

My Thoughts & Results: _____

_____

_____

_____

_____

_____

_____

_____

_____

_____

_____

_____

_____

_____

_____

Today's Date: _____ *I'm Feeling:* _____

Frequency Exercise: _____

_____

_____

_____

_____

_____

_____

_____

_____

_____

My Thoughts & Results: _____

_____

_____

_____

_____

_____

_____

_____

_____

_____

_____

_____

_____

_____

Today's Date: _____ *I'm Feeling:* _____

Frequency Exercise: _____

_____

_____

_____

_____

_____

_____

_____

_____

_____

My Thoughts & Results: _____

_____

_____

_____

_____

_____

_____

_____

_____

_____

_____

_____

_____

_____

Today's Date: _____I'm Feeling: _____

Frequency Exercise: _____

_____

_____

_____

_____

_____

_____

_____

_____

_____

My Thoughts & Results: _____

_____

_____

_____

_____

_____

_____

_____

_____

_____

_____

_____

_____

Today's Date: _____ *I'm Feeling:* _____

Frequency Exercise: _____

_____

_____

_____

_____

_____

_____

_____

_____

_____

My Thoughts & Results: _____

_____

_____

_____

_____

_____

_____

_____

_____

_____

_____

_____

_____

_____

Today's Date: _____ *I'm Feeling:* _____

Frequency Exercise: _____

_____

_____

_____

_____

_____

_____

_____

_____

_____

_____

My Thoughts & Results: _____

_____

_____

_____

_____

_____

_____

_____

_____

_____

_____

_____

_____

_____

Today's Date: _____ *I'm Feeling:* _____

Frequency Exercise: _____

_____

_____

_____

_____

_____

_____

_____

_____

_____

My Thoughts & Results: _____

_____

_____

_____

_____

_____

_____

_____

_____

_____

_____

_____

_____

_____

Today's Date: _____*I'm Feeling:* _____

Frequency Exercise: _____

_____

_____

_____

_____

_____

_____

_____

_____

_____

My Thoughts & Results: _____

_____

_____

_____

_____

_____

_____

_____

_____

_____

_____

_____

_____

_____

Today's Date: _____ *I'm Feeling:* _____

Frequency Exercise: _____

_____

_____

_____

_____

_____

_____

_____

_____

_____

My Thoughts & Results: _____

_____

_____

_____

_____

_____

_____

_____

_____

_____

_____

_____

_____

_____

_____

Today's Date: _____ *I'm Feeling:* _____

Frequency Exercise: _____

_____

_____

_____

_____

_____

_____

_____

_____

_____

My Thoughts & Results: _____

_____

_____

_____

_____

_____

_____

_____

_____

_____

_____

_____

_____

_____

Today's Date: _____ *I'm Feeling:* _____

Frequency Exercise: _____

_____

_____

_____

_____

_____

_____

_____

_____

_____

My Thoughts & Results: _____

_____

_____

_____

_____

_____

_____

_____

_____

_____

_____

_____

_____

_____

_____

Today's Date: _____ *I'm Feeling:* _____

Frequency Exercise: _____

_____

_____

_____

_____

_____

_____

_____

_____

_____

My Thoughts & Results: _____

_____

_____

_____

_____

_____

_____

_____

_____

_____

_____

_____

_____

_____

Today's Date: _____ *I'm Feeling:* _____

Frequency Exercise: _____

_____

_____

_____

_____

_____

_____

_____

_____

_____

My Thoughts & Results: _____

_____

_____

_____

_____

_____

_____

_____

_____

_____

_____

_____

_____

_____

Today's Date: _____I'm Feeling: _____

Frequency Exercise: _____

_____

_____

_____

_____

_____

_____

_____

_____

My Thoughts & Results: _____

_____

_____

_____

_____

_____

_____

_____

_____

_____

_____

_____

Today's Date: _____ I'm Feeling: _____

Frequency Exercise: _____

_____

_____

_____

_____

_____

_____

_____

_____

_____

My Thoughts & Results: _____

_____

_____

_____

_____

_____

_____

_____

_____

_____

_____

_____

_____

_____

Today's Date: _____I'm Feeling: _____

Frequency Exercise: _____

_____

_____

_____

_____

_____

_____

_____

_____

_____

My Thoughts & Results: _____

_____

_____

_____

_____

_____

_____

_____

_____

_____

_____

_____

_____

Today's Date: _____*I'm Feeling:* _____

Frequency Exercise: _____

_____

_____

_____

_____

_____

_____

_____

_____

_____

My Thoughts & Results: _____

_____

_____

_____

_____

_____

_____

_____

_____

_____

_____

_____

_____

_____

Today's Date: _____ I'm Feeling: _____

Frequency Exercise: _____

_____

_____

_____

_____

_____

_____

_____

_____

_____

My Thoughts & Results: _____

_____

_____

_____

_____

_____

_____

_____

_____

_____

_____

_____

_____

Today's Date: _____*I'm Feeling:* _____

Frequency Exercise: _____

_____

_____

_____

_____

_____

_____

_____

_____

_____

My Thoughts & Results: _____

_____

_____

_____

_____

_____

_____

_____

_____

_____

_____

_____

_____

_____

Today's Date: _____ *I'm Feeling:* _____

Frequency Exercise: _____

_____

_____

_____

_____

_____

_____

_____

_____

My Thoughts & Results: _____

_____

_____

_____

_____

_____

_____

_____

_____

_____

_____

_____

_____

Today's Date: _____ *I'm Feeling:* _____

Frequency Exercise: _____

_____

_____

_____

_____

_____

_____

_____

_____

_____

My Thoughts & Results: _____

_____

_____

_____

_____

_____

_____

_____

_____

_____

_____

_____

_____

_____

_____

Today's Date: _____ *I'm Feeling:* _____

Frequency Exercise: _____

_____

_____

_____

_____

_____

_____

_____

_____

_____

My Thoughts & Results: _____

_____

_____

_____

_____

_____

_____

_____

_____

_____

_____

_____

_____

_____

Today's Date: _____ *I'm Feeling:* _____

Frequency Exercise: _____

_____

_____

_____

_____

_____

_____

_____

_____

_____

My Thoughts & Results: _____

_____

_____

_____

_____

_____

_____

_____

_____

_____

_____

_____

_____

_____

_____

Today's Date: _____ *I'm Feeling:* _____

Frequency Exercise: _____

_____

_____

_____

_____

_____

_____

_____

_____

_____

_____

My Thoughts & Results: _____

_____

_____

_____

_____

_____

_____

_____

_____

_____

_____

_____

_____

_____

Today's Date: _____ I'm Feeling: _____

Frequency Exercise: _____

_____

_____

_____

_____

_____

_____

_____

_____

_____

My Thoughts & Results: _____

_____

_____

_____

_____

_____

_____

_____

_____

_____

_____

_____

_____

Today's Date: _____ I'm Feeling: _____

Frequency Exercise: _____

_____

_____

_____

_____

_____

_____

_____

_____

_____

My Thoughts & Results: _____

_____

_____

_____

_____

_____

_____

_____

_____

_____

_____

_____

_____

Today's Date: _____I'm Feeling: _____

Frequency Exercise: _____

_____

_____

_____

_____

_____

_____

_____

_____

_____

My Thoughts & Results: _____

_____

_____

_____

_____

_____

_____

_____

_____

_____

_____

_____

_____

_____

_____

Today's Date: _____*I'm Feeling:* _____

Frequency Exercise: _____

_____

_____

_____

_____

_____

_____

_____

_____

My Thoughts & Results: _____

_____

_____

_____

_____

_____

_____

_____

_____

_____

_____

_____

_____

Today's Date: _____ *I'm Feeling:* _____

Frequency Exercise: _____

_____

_____

_____

_____

_____

_____

_____

_____

_____

My Thoughts & Results: _____

_____

_____

_____

_____

_____

_____

_____

_____

_____

_____

_____

_____

_____

_____

Today's Date: _____I'm Feeling: _____

Frequency Exercise: _____

_____

_____

_____

_____

_____

_____

_____

_____

_____

_____

My Thoughts & Results: _____

_____

_____

_____

_____

_____

_____

_____

_____

_____

_____

_____

_____

_____

Today's Date: _____*I'm Feeling:* _____

Frequency Exercise: _____

_____

_____

_____

_____

_____

_____

_____

_____

_____

My Thoughts & Results: _____

_____

_____

_____

_____

_____

_____

_____

_____

_____

_____

_____

_____

_____

Today's Date: _____*I'm Feeling:* _____

Frequency Exercise: _____

_____

_____

_____

_____

_____

_____

_____

_____

_____

My Thoughts & Results: _____

_____

_____

_____

_____

_____

_____

_____

_____

_____

_____

_____

_____

_____

Today's Date: _____ I'm Feeling: _____

Frequency Exercise: _____

_____

_____

_____

_____

_____

_____

_____

_____

_____

_____

My Thoughts & Results: _____

_____

_____

_____

_____

_____

_____

_____

_____

_____

_____

_____

_____

_____

_____

Today's Date: _____ *I'm Feeling:* _____

Frequency Exercise: _____

_____

_____

_____

_____

_____

_____

_____

_____

My Thoughts & Results: _____

_____

_____

_____

_____

_____

_____

_____

_____

_____

_____

_____

_____

Today's Date: _____ *I'm Feeling:* _____

Frequency Exercise: _____

_____

_____

_____

_____

_____

_____

_____

_____

_____

My Thoughts & Results: _____

_____

_____

_____

_____

_____

_____

_____

_____

_____

_____

_____

_____

_____

Today's Date: _____ I'm Feeling: _____

Frequency Exercise: _____

_____

_____

_____

_____

_____

_____

_____

_____

_____

My Thoughts & Results: _____

_____

_____

_____

_____

_____

_____

_____

_____

_____

_____

_____

_____

_____

Today's Date: _____ *I'm Feeling:* _____

Frequency Exercise: _____

_____

_____

_____

_____

_____

_____

_____

_____

My Thoughts & Results: _____

_____

_____

_____

_____

_____

_____

_____

_____

_____

_____

_____

_____

_____

Today's Date: _____ *I'm Feeling:* _____

Frequency Exercise: _____

_____

_____

_____

_____

_____

_____

_____

_____

_____

My Thoughts & Results: _____

_____

_____

_____

_____

_____

_____

_____

_____

_____

_____

_____

_____

Today's Date: _____ *I'm Feeling:* _____

Frequency Exercise: _____

_____

_____

_____

_____

_____

_____

_____

_____

_____

My Thoughts & Results: _____

_____

_____

_____

_____

_____

_____

_____

_____

_____

_____

_____

_____

_____

_____

Today's Date: _____ *I'm Feeling:* _____

Frequency Exercise: _____

_____

_____

_____

_____

_____

_____

_____

_____

My Thoughts & Results: _____

_____

_____

_____

_____

_____

_____

_____

_____

_____

_____

_____

_____

Today's Date: _____ *I'm Feeling:* _____

Frequency Exercise: _____

_____

_____

_____

_____

_____

_____

_____

_____

_____

My Thoughts & Results: _____

_____

_____

_____

_____

_____

_____

_____

_____

_____

_____

_____

_____

_____

Today's Date: _____ I'm Feeling: _____

Frequency Exercise: _____

_____

_____

_____

_____

_____

_____

_____

_____

_____

My Thoughts & Results: _____

_____

_____

_____

_____

_____

_____

_____

_____

_____

_____

_____

_____

Today's Date: _____ I'm Feeling: _____

Frequency Exercise: _____

_____

_____

_____

_____

_____

_____

_____

_____

_____

My Thoughts & Results: _____

_____

_____

_____

_____

_____

_____

_____

_____

_____

_____

_____

_____

Today's Date: _____I'm Feeling: _____

Frequency Exercise: _____

_____

_____

_____

_____

_____

_____

_____

_____

My Thoughts & Results: _____

_____

_____

_____

_____

_____

_____

_____

_____

_____

_____

_____

Today's Date: _____*I'm Feeling:* _____

Frequency Exercise: _____

_____

_____

_____

_____

_____

_____

_____

_____

_____

My Thoughts & Results: _____

_____

_____

_____

_____

_____

_____

_____

_____

_____

_____

_____

_____

_____

_____

Today's Date: _____ *I'm Feeling:* _____

Frequency Exercise: _____

_____

_____

_____

_____

_____

_____

_____

_____

_____

My Thoughts & Results: _____

_____

_____

_____

_____

_____

_____

_____

_____

_____

_____

_____

_____

_____

Today's Date: _____ *I'm Feeling:* _____

Frequency Exercise: _____

_____

_____

_____

_____

_____

_____

_____

_____

_____

My Thoughts & Results: _____

_____

_____

_____

_____

_____

_____

_____

_____

_____

_____

_____

_____

_____

Today's Date: _____I'm Feeling: _____

Frequency Exercise: _____

_____

_____

_____

_____

_____

_____

_____

_____

_____

_____

My Thoughts & Results: _____

_____

_____

_____

_____

_____

_____

_____

_____

_____

_____

_____

_____

_____

_____

Today's Date: _____ *I'm Feeling:* _____

Frequency Exercise: _____

_____

_____

_____

_____

_____

_____

_____

_____

_____

My Thoughts & Results: _____

_____

_____

_____

_____

_____

_____

_____

_____

_____

_____

_____

_____

_____

Today's Date: _____ I'm Feeling: _____

Frequency Exercise: _____

_____

_____

_____

_____

_____

_____

_____

_____

My Thoughts & Results: _____

_____

_____

_____

_____

_____

_____

_____

_____

_____

_____

_____

Today's Date: _____ *I'm Feeling:* _____

Frequency Exercise: _____

_____

_____

_____

_____

_____

_____

_____

_____

_____

My Thoughts & Results: _____

_____

_____

_____

_____

_____

_____

_____

_____

_____

_____

_____

_____

_____

Today's Date: _____ I'm Feeling: _____

Frequency Exercise: _____

_____

_____

_____

_____

_____

_____

_____

_____

_____

My Thoughts & Results: _____

_____

_____

_____

_____

_____

_____

_____

_____

_____

_____

_____

_____

Today's Date: _____I'm Feeling: _____

Frequency Exercise: _____

_____

_____

_____

_____

_____

_____

_____

_____

_____

_____

My Thoughts & Results: _____

_____

_____

_____

_____

_____

_____

_____

_____

_____

_____

_____

_____

_____

_____

Today's Date: _____ *I'm Feeling:* _____

Frequency Exercise: _____

_____

_____

_____

_____

_____

_____

_____

_____

_____

My Thoughts & Results: _____

_____

_____

_____

_____

_____

_____

_____

_____

_____

_____

_____

_____

Today's Date: _____*I'm Feeling:* _____

Frequency Exercise: _____

_____

_____

_____

_____

_____

_____

_____

_____

_____

My Thoughts & Results: _____

_____

_____

_____

_____

_____

_____

_____

_____

_____

_____

_____

_____

_____

Today's Date: _____ I'm Feeling: _____

Frequency Exercise: _____

_____

_____

_____

_____

_____

_____

_____

_____

_____

My Thoughts & Results: _____

_____

_____

_____

_____

_____

_____

_____

_____

_____

_____

_____

_____

Today's Date: _____I'm Feeling: _____

Frequency Exercise: _____

_____

_____

_____

_____

_____

_____

_____

_____

_____

My Thoughts & Results: _____

_____

_____

_____

_____

_____

_____

_____

_____

_____

_____

_____

_____

_____

Today's Date: _____ *I'm Feeling:* _____

Frequency Exercise: _____

_____

_____

_____

_____

_____

_____

_____

_____

_____

My Thoughts & Results: _____

_____

_____

_____

_____

_____

_____

_____

_____

_____

_____

_____

_____

_____

Today's Date: _____ *I'm Feeling:* _____

Frequency Exercise: _____

_____

_____

_____

_____

_____

_____

_____

_____

_____

My Thoughts & Results: _____

_____

_____

_____

_____

_____

_____

_____

_____

_____

_____

_____

_____

_____

_____

Today's Date: _____ *I'm Feeling:* _____

Frequency Exercise: _____

_____

_____

_____

_____

_____

_____

_____

_____

_____

My Thoughts & Results: _____

_____

_____

_____

_____

_____

_____

_____

_____

_____

_____

_____

_____

Today's Date: _____I'm Feeling: _____

Frequency Exercise: _____

_____

_____

_____

_____

_____

_____

_____

_____

_____

My Thoughts & Results: _____

_____

_____

_____

_____

_____

_____

_____

_____

_____

_____

_____

_____

_____

Today's Date: _____ I'm Feeling: _____

Frequency Exercise: _____

_____

_____

_____

_____

_____

_____

_____

_____

_____

My Thoughts & Results: _____

_____

_____

_____

_____

_____

_____

_____

_____

_____

_____

_____

_____

_____

Today's Date: _____*I'm Feeling:* _____

Frequency Exercise: _____

_____

_____

_____

_____

_____

_____

_____

_____

_____

My Thoughts & Results: _____

_____

_____

_____

_____

_____

_____

_____

_____

_____

_____

_____

_____

_____

Today's Date: _____*I'm Feeling:* _____

Frequency Exercise: _____

_____

_____

_____

_____

_____

_____

_____

_____

My Thoughts & Results: _____

_____

_____

_____

_____

_____

_____

_____

_____

_____

_____

_____

_____

Today's Date: _____ *I'm Feeling:* _____

Frequency Exercise: _____

_____

_____

_____

_____

_____

_____

_____

_____

_____

My Thoughts & Results: _____

_____

_____

_____

_____

_____

_____

_____

_____

_____

_____

_____

_____

_____

Today's Date: _____ *I'm Feeling:* _____

Frequency Exercise: _____

_____

_____

_____

_____

_____

_____

_____

_____

_____

My Thoughts & Results: _____

_____

_____

_____

_____

_____

_____

_____

_____

_____

_____

_____

_____

_____

Today's Date: _____I'm Feeling: _____

Frequency Exercise: _____

_____

_____

_____

_____

_____

_____

_____

_____

_____

_____

My Thoughts & Results: _____

_____

_____

_____

_____

_____

_____

_____

_____

_____

_____

_____

_____

_____

Today's Date: _____ *I'm Feeling:* _____

Frequency Exercise: _____

_____

_____

_____

_____

_____

_____

_____

_____

_____

My Thoughts & Results: _____

_____

_____

_____

_____

_____

_____

_____

_____

_____

_____

_____

_____

_____

_____

Today's Date: _____ *I'm Feeling:* _____

Frequency Exercise: _____

_____

_____

_____

_____

_____

_____

_____

_____

_____

My Thoughts & Results: _____

_____

_____

_____

_____

_____

_____

_____

_____

_____

_____

_____

_____

_____

Today's Date: _____ I'm Feeling: _____

Frequency Exercise: _____

_____

_____

_____

_____

_____

_____

_____

_____

_____

My Thoughts & Results: _____

_____

_____

_____

_____

_____

_____

_____

_____

_____

_____

_____

_____

_____

Today's Date: _____ *I'm Feeling:* _____

Frequency Exercise: _____

_____

_____

_____

_____

_____

_____

_____

_____

My Thoughts & Results: _____

_____

_____

_____

_____

_____

_____

_____

_____

_____

_____

_____

_____

Today's Date: _____*I'm Feeling:* _____

Frequency Exercise: _____

_____

_____

_____

_____

_____

_____

_____

_____

_____

My Thoughts & Results: _____

_____

_____

_____

_____

_____

_____

_____

_____

_____

_____

_____

_____

_____

Today's Date: _____*I'm Feeling:* _____

Frequency Exercise: _____

_____

_____

_____

_____

_____

_____

_____

_____

_____

My Thoughts & Results: _____

_____

_____

_____

_____

_____

_____

_____

_____

_____

_____

_____

_____

_____

Today's Date: _____ I'm Feeling: _____

Frequency Exercise: _____

_____

_____

_____

_____

_____

_____

_____

_____

My Thoughts & Results: _____

_____

_____

_____

_____

_____

_____

_____

_____

_____

_____

_____

_____

_____

Today's Date: _____*I'm Feeling:* _____

Frequency Exercise: _____

_____

_____

_____

_____

_____

_____

_____

_____

_____

My Thoughts & Results: _____

_____

_____

_____

_____

_____

_____

_____

_____

_____

_____

_____

_____

_____

Today's Date: _____ I'm Feeling: _____

Frequency Exercise: _____

_____

_____

_____

_____

_____

_____

_____

_____

_____

My Thoughts & Results: _____

_____

_____

_____

_____

_____

_____

_____

_____

_____

_____

_____

_____

_____

Today's Date: _____*I'm Feeling:* _____

Frequency Exercise: _____

_____

_____

_____

_____

_____

_____

_____

_____

_____

My Thoughts & Results: _____

_____

_____

_____

_____

_____

_____

_____

_____

_____

_____

_____

_____

_____

Today's Date: _____ *I'm Feeling:* _____

Frequency Exercise: _____

_____

_____

_____

_____

_____

_____

_____

_____

_____

My Thoughts & Results: _____

_____

_____

_____

_____

_____

_____

_____

_____

_____

_____

_____

_____

_____

Today's Date: _____ *I'm Feeling:* _____

Frequency Exercise: _____

_____

_____

_____

_____

_____

_____

_____

_____

_____

My Thoughts & Results: _____

_____

_____

_____

_____

_____

_____

_____

_____

_____

_____

_____

_____

Today's Date: _____I'm Feeling: _____

Frequency Exercise: _____

_____

_____

_____

_____

_____

_____

_____

_____

_____

My Thoughts & Results: _____

_____

_____

_____

_____

_____

_____

_____

_____

_____

_____

_____

_____

_____

Today's Date: _____ *I'm Feeling:* _____

Frequency Exercise: _____

_____

_____

_____

_____

_____

_____

_____

_____

_____

My Thoughts & Results: _____

_____

_____

_____

_____

_____

_____

_____

_____

_____

_____

_____

_____

_____

_____

Today's Date: _____ *I'm Feeling:* _____

Frequency Exercise: _____

_____

_____

_____

_____

_____

_____

_____

_____

_____

My Thoughts & Results: _____

_____

_____

_____

_____

_____

_____

_____

_____

_____

_____

_____

_____

_____

Today's Date: _____*I'm Feeling:* _____

Frequency Exercise: _____

_____

_____

_____

_____

_____

_____

_____

_____

_____

_____

My Thoughts & Results: _____

_____

_____

_____

_____

_____

_____

_____

_____

_____

_____

_____

_____

_____

Today's Date: _____I'm Feeling: _____

Frequency Exercise: _____

_____

_____

_____

_____

_____

_____

_____

_____

_____

My Thoughts & Results: _____

_____

_____

_____

_____

_____

_____

_____

_____

_____

_____

_____

_____

Today's Date: _____*I'm Feeling:* _____

Frequency Exercise: _____

_____

_____

_____

_____

_____

_____

_____

_____

_____

_____

My Thoughts & Results: _____

_____

_____

_____

_____

_____

_____

_____

_____

_____

_____

_____

_____

_____

_____

Today's Date: _____ I'm Feeling: _____

Frequency Exercise: _____

_____

_____

_____

_____

_____

_____

_____

_____

_____

My Thoughts & Results: _____

_____

_____

_____

_____

_____

_____

_____

_____

_____

_____

_____

_____

Today's Date: _____ *I'm Feeling:* _____

Frequency Exercise: _____

_____

_____

_____

_____

_____

_____

_____

_____

_____

My Thoughts & Results: _____

_____

_____

_____

_____

_____

_____

_____

_____

_____

_____

_____

_____

Today's Date: _____ *I'm Feeling:* _____

Frequency Exercise: _____

_____

_____

_____

_____

_____

_____

_____

_____

_____

My Thoughts & Results: _____

_____

_____

_____

_____

_____

_____

_____

_____

_____

_____

_____

_____

_____

Today's Date: _____ *I'm Feeling:* _____

Frequency Exercise: _____

_____

_____

_____

_____

_____

_____

_____

_____

_____

_____

My Thoughts & Results: _____

_____

_____

_____

_____

_____

_____

_____

_____

_____

_____

_____

_____

_____

Today's Date: _____ *I'm Feeling:* _____

Frequency Exercise: _____

_____

_____

_____

_____

_____

_____

_____

_____

My Thoughts & Results: _____

_____

_____

_____

_____

_____

_____

_____

_____

_____

_____

_____

_____

Today's Date: _____ *I'm Feeling:* _____

Frequency Exercise: _____

_____

_____

_____

_____

_____

_____

_____

_____

_____

My Thoughts & Results: _____

_____

_____

_____

_____

_____

_____

_____

_____

_____

_____

_____

_____

_____

Today's Date: _____ I'm Feeling: _____

Frequency Exercise: _____

_____

_____

_____

_____

_____

_____

_____

_____

_____

My Thoughts & Results: _____

_____

_____

_____

_____

_____

_____

_____

_____

_____

_____

_____

_____

Today's Date: _____ *I'm Feeling:* _____

Frequency Exercise: _____

_____

_____

_____

_____

_____

_____

_____

_____

_____

My Thoughts & Results: _____

_____

_____

_____

_____

_____

_____

_____

_____

_____

_____

_____

_____

_____

Today's Date: _____I'm Feeling: _____

Frequency Exercise: _____

_____

_____

_____

_____

_____

_____

_____

_____

_____

My Thoughts & Results: _____

_____

_____

_____

_____

_____

_____

_____

_____

_____

_____

_____

_____

_____

_____

Today's Date: _____ *I'm Feeling:* _____

Frequency Exercise: _____

_____

_____

_____

_____

_____

_____

_____

_____

_____

My Thoughts & Results: _____

_____

_____

_____

_____

_____

_____

_____

_____

_____

_____

_____

_____

Today's Date: _____I'm Feeling: _____

Frequency Exercise: _____

_____

_____

_____

_____

_____

_____

_____

_____

_____

My Thoughts & Results: _____

_____

_____

_____

_____

_____

_____

_____

_____

_____

_____

_____

_____

Today's Date: _____ *I'm Feeling:* _____

Frequency Exercise: _____

_____

_____

_____

_____

_____

_____

_____

_____

_____

My Thoughts & Results: _____

_____

_____

_____

_____

_____

_____

_____

_____

_____

_____

_____

_____

_____

Today's Date: _____I'm Feeling: _____

Frequency Exercise: _____

_____

_____

_____

_____

_____

_____

_____

_____

_____

My Thoughts & Results: _____

_____

_____

_____

_____

_____

_____

_____

_____

_____

_____

_____

_____

Today's Date: _____ *I'm Feeling:* _____

Frequency Exercise: _____

_____

_____

_____

_____

_____

_____

_____

_____

_____

My Thoughts & Results: _____

_____

_____

_____

_____

_____

_____

_____

_____

_____

_____

_____

_____

_____

Today's Date: _____*I'm Feeling:* _____

Frequency Exercise: _____

_____

_____

_____

_____

_____

_____

_____

_____

_____

My Thoughts & Results: _____

_____

_____

_____

_____

_____

_____

_____

_____

_____

_____

_____

_____

_____

_____

Today's Date: _____*I'm Feeling:* _____

Frequency Exercise: _____

_____

_____

_____

_____

_____

_____

_____

_____

_____

My Thoughts & Results: _____

_____

_____

_____

_____

_____

_____

_____

_____

_____

_____

_____

_____

_____

Today's Date: _____ *I'm Feeling:* _____

Frequency Exercise: _____

_____

_____

_____

_____

_____

_____

_____

_____

_____

My Thoughts & Results: _____

_____

_____

_____

_____

_____

_____

_____

_____

_____

_____

_____

_____

_____

Today's Date: _____I'm Feeling: _____

Frequency Exercise: _____

_____

_____

_____

_____

_____

_____

_____

_____

_____

My Thoughts & Results: _____

_____

_____

_____

_____

_____

_____

_____

_____

_____

_____

_____

_____

_____

Today's Date: _____I'm Feeling: _____

Frequency Exercise: _____

_____

_____

_____

_____

_____

_____

_____

_____

_____

My Thoughts & Results: _____

_____

_____

_____

_____

_____

_____

_____

_____

_____

_____

_____

_____

Today's Date: _____ I'm Feeling: _____

Frequency Exercise: _____

_____

_____

_____

_____

_____

_____

_____

_____

_____

My Thoughts & Results: _____

_____

_____

_____

_____

_____

_____

_____

_____

_____

_____

_____

_____

_____

Today's Date: _____ *I'm Feeling:* _____

Frequency Exercise: _____

_____

_____

_____

_____

_____

_____

_____

_____

_____

_____

My Thoughts & Results: _____

_____

_____

_____

_____

_____

_____

_____

_____

_____

_____

_____

_____

_____

_____

Today's Date: _____ *I'm Feeling:* _____

Frequency Exercise: _____

_____

_____

_____

_____

_____

_____

_____

_____

_____

My Thoughts & Results: _____

_____

_____

_____

_____

_____

_____

_____

_____

_____

_____

_____

_____

_____

Today's Date: _____*I'm Feeling:* _____

Frequency Exercise: _____

_____

_____

_____

_____

_____

_____

_____

_____

_____

My Thoughts & Results: _____

_____

_____

_____

_____

_____

_____

_____

_____

_____

_____

_____

_____

_____

Today's Date: _____ *I'm Feeling:* _____

Frequency Exercise: _____

_____

_____

_____

_____

_____

_____

_____

_____

_____

My Thoughts & Results: _____

_____

_____

_____

_____

_____

_____

_____

_____

_____

_____

_____

_____

_____

_____

Today's Date: _____ I'm Feeling: _____

Frequency Exercise: _____

_____

_____

_____

_____

_____

_____

_____

_____

_____

My Thoughts & Results: _____

_____

_____

_____

_____

_____

_____

_____

_____

_____

_____

_____

_____

_____

Today's Date: _____ *I'm Feeling:* _____

Frequency Exercise: _____

_____

_____

_____

_____

_____

_____

_____

_____

_____

My Thoughts & Results: _____

_____

_____

_____

_____

_____

_____

_____

_____

_____

_____

_____

_____

_____

_____

Today's Date: _____*I'm Feeling:* _____

Frequency Exercise: _____

_____

_____

_____

_____

_____

_____

_____

_____

_____

My Thoughts & Results: _____

_____

_____

_____

_____

_____

_____

_____

_____

_____

_____

_____

_____

_____

Today's Date: _____I'm Feeling: _____

Frequency Exercise: _____

_____

_____

_____

_____

_____

_____

_____

_____

_____

My Thoughts & Results: _____

_____

_____

_____

_____

_____

_____

_____

_____

_____

_____

_____

_____

_____

Today's Date: _____I'm Feeling: _____

Frequency Exercise: _____

_____

_____

_____

_____

_____

_____

_____

_____

_____

My Thoughts & Results: _____

_____

_____

_____

_____

_____

_____

_____

_____

_____

_____

_____

_____

_____

Today's Date: _____I'm Feeling: _____

Frequency Exercise: _____

_____

_____

_____

_____

_____

_____

_____

_____

_____

My Thoughts & Results: _____

_____

_____

_____

_____

_____

_____

_____

_____

_____

_____

_____

_____

_____

Today's Date: _____*I'm Feeling:* _____

Frequency Exercise: _____

_____

_____

_____

_____

_____

_____

_____

_____

_____

My Thoughts & Results: _____

_____

_____

_____

_____

_____

_____

_____

_____

_____

_____

_____

_____

_____

Today's Date: _____ *I'm Feeling:* _____

Frequency Exercise: _____

_____

_____

_____

_____

_____

_____

_____

_____

_____

My Thoughts & Results: _____

_____

_____

_____

_____

_____

_____

_____

_____

_____

_____

_____

_____

_____

Today's Date: _____ I'm Feeling: _____

Frequency Exercise: _____

_____

_____

_____

_____

_____

_____

_____

_____

_____

My Thoughts & Results: _____

_____

_____

_____

_____

_____

_____

_____

_____

_____

_____

_____

_____

_____

Today's Date: _____I'm Feeling: _____

Frequency Exercise: _____

_____

_____

_____

_____

_____

_____

_____

_____

_____

_____

My Thoughts & Results: _____

_____

_____

_____

_____

_____

_____

_____

_____

_____

_____

_____

_____

_____

_____

_____

Today's Date: _____I'm Feeling: _____

Frequency Exercise: _____

_____

_____

_____

_____

_____

_____

_____

_____

_____

My Thoughts & Results: _____

_____

_____

_____

_____

_____

_____

_____

_____

_____

_____

_____

_____

Today's Date: _____I'm Feeling: _____

Frequency Exercise: _____

_____

_____

_____

_____

_____

_____

_____

_____

_____

My Thoughts & Results: _____

_____

_____

_____

_____

_____

_____

_____

_____

_____

_____

_____

_____

_____

Today's Date: _____I'm Feeling: _____

Frequency Exercise: _____

_____

_____

_____

_____

_____

_____

_____

_____

My Thoughts & Results: _____

_____

_____

_____

_____

_____

_____

_____

_____

_____

_____

_____

_____

Today's Date: _____I'm Feeling: _____

Frequency Exercise: _____

_____

_____

_____

_____

_____

_____

_____

_____

_____

My Thoughts & Results: _____

_____

_____

_____

_____

_____

_____

_____

_____

_____

_____

_____

_____

_____

_____

Today's Date: _____ *I'm Feeling:* _____

Frequency Exercise: _____

_____

_____

_____

_____

_____

_____

_____

_____

_____

My Thoughts & Results: _____

_____

_____

_____

_____

_____

_____

_____

_____

_____

_____

_____

_____

_____

Today's Date: _____ I'm Feeling: _____

Frequency Exercise: _____

_____

_____

_____

_____

_____

_____

_____

_____

_____

My Thoughts & Results: _____

_____

_____

_____

_____

_____

_____

_____

_____

_____

_____

_____

_____

_____

_____

Today's Date: _____ *I'm Feeling:* _____

Frequency Exercise: _____

_____

_____

_____

_____

_____

_____

_____

_____

_____

My Thoughts & Results: _____

_____

_____

_____

_____

_____

_____

_____

_____

_____

_____

_____

_____

_____

Today's Date: _____*I'm Feeling:* _____

Frequency Exercise: _____

_____

_____

_____

_____

_____

_____

_____

_____

_____

My Thoughts & Results: _____

_____

_____

_____

_____

_____

_____

_____

_____

_____

_____

_____

_____

_____

Today's Date: _____ I'm Feeling: _____

Frequency Exercise: _____

_____

_____

_____

_____

_____

_____

_____

_____

My Thoughts & Results: _____

_____

_____

_____

_____

_____

_____

_____

_____

_____

_____

_____

Today's Date: _____I'm Feeling: _____

Frequency Exercise: _____

_____

_____

_____

_____

_____

_____

_____

_____

_____

My Thoughts & Results: _____

_____

_____

_____

_____

_____

_____

_____

_____

_____

_____

_____

_____

_____

Today's Date: _____ *I'm Feeling:* _____

Frequency Exercise: _____

_____

_____

_____

_____

_____

_____

_____

_____

_____

My Thoughts & Results: _____

_____

_____

_____

_____

_____

_____

_____

_____

_____

_____

_____

_____

_____

Today's Date: _____ *I'm Feeling:* _____

Frequency Exercise: _____

_____

_____

_____

_____

_____

_____

_____

_____

_____

My Thoughts & Results: _____

_____

_____

_____

_____

_____

_____

_____

_____

_____

_____

_____

_____

_____

_____

Today's Date: _____ *I'm Feeling:* _____

Frequency Exercise: _____

_____

_____

_____

_____

_____

_____

_____

_____

_____

My Thoughts & Results: _____

_____

_____

_____

_____

_____

_____

_____

_____

_____

_____

_____

_____

_____

_____

Today's Date: _____ *I'm Feeling:* _____

Frequency Exercise: _____

_____

_____

_____

_____

_____

_____

_____

_____

_____

My Thoughts & Results: _____

_____

_____

_____

_____

_____

_____

_____

_____

_____

_____

_____

_____

Today's Date: _____ I'm Feeling: _____

Frequency Exercise: _____

_____

_____

_____

_____

_____

_____

_____

_____

My Thoughts & Results: _____

_____

_____

_____

_____

_____

_____

_____

_____

_____

_____

_____

Today's Date: _____*I'm Feeling:* _____

Frequency Exercise: _____

_____

_____

_____

_____

_____

_____

_____

_____

_____

My Thoughts & Results: _____

_____

_____

_____

_____

_____

_____

_____

_____

_____

_____

_____

_____

_____

Today's Date: _____*I'm Feeling:* _____

Frequency Exercise: _____

_____

_____

_____

_____

_____

_____

_____

_____

_____

My Thoughts & Results: _____

_____

_____

_____

_____

_____

_____

_____

_____

_____

_____

_____

_____

_____

Today's Date: _____ I'm Feeling: _____

Frequency Exercise: _____

_____

_____

_____

_____

_____

_____

_____

_____

_____

My Thoughts & Results: _____

_____

_____

_____

_____

_____

_____

_____

_____

_____

_____

_____

_____

_____

Today's Date: _____I'm Feeling: _____

Frequency Exercise: _____

_____

_____

_____

_____

_____

_____

_____

_____

_____

My Thoughts & Results: _____

_____

_____

_____

_____

_____

_____

_____

_____

_____

_____

_____

_____

_____

Today's Date: _____*I'm Feeling:* _____

Frequency Exercise: _____

_____

_____

_____

_____

_____

_____

_____

_____

_____

My Thoughts & Results: _____

_____

_____

_____

_____

_____

_____

_____

_____

_____

_____

_____

_____

_____

_____

Today's Date: _____*I'm Feeling:* _____

Frequency Exercise: _____

_____

_____

_____

_____

_____

_____

_____

_____

_____

My Thoughts & Results: _____

_____

_____

_____

_____

_____

_____

_____

_____

_____

_____

_____

_____

Today's Date: _____ *I'm Feeling:* _____

Frequency Exercise: _____

_____

_____

_____

_____

_____

_____

_____

_____

_____

My Thoughts & Results: _____

_____

_____

_____

_____

_____

_____

_____

_____

_____

_____

_____

_____

_____

_____

Today's Date: _____ *I'm Feeling:* _____

Frequency Exercise: _____

_____

_____

_____

_____

_____

_____

_____

_____

_____

My Thoughts & Results: _____

_____

_____

_____

_____

_____

_____

_____

_____

_____

_____

_____

_____

_____

_____

Today's Date: _____ *I'm Feeling:* _____

Frequency Exercise: _____

_____

_____

_____

_____

_____

_____

_____

_____

_____

My Thoughts & Results: _____

_____

_____

_____

_____

_____

_____

_____

_____

_____

_____

_____

_____

_____

Today's Date: _____ *I'm Feeling:* _____

Frequency Exercise: _____

_____

_____

_____

_____

_____

_____

_____

_____

_____

My Thoughts & Results: _____

_____

_____

_____

_____

_____

_____

_____

_____

_____

_____

_____

_____

_____

Today's Date: _____*I'm Feeling:* _____

Frequency Exercise: _____

_____

_____

_____

_____

_____

_____

_____

_____

_____

My Thoughts & Results: _____

_____

_____

_____

_____

_____

_____

_____

_____

_____

_____

_____

_____

_____

Today's Date: _____ I'm Feeling: _____

Frequency Exercise: _____

_____

_____

_____

_____

_____

_____

_____

_____

My Thoughts & Results: _____

_____

_____

_____

_____

_____

_____

_____

_____

_____

_____

_____

_____

Today's Date: _____ I'm Feeling: _____

Frequency Exercise: _____

_____

_____

_____

_____

_____

_____

_____

_____

_____

My Thoughts & Results: _____

_____

_____

_____

_____

_____

_____

_____

_____

_____

_____

_____

_____

_____

Today's Date: _____*I'm Feeling:* _____

Frequency Exercise: _____

_____

_____

_____

_____

_____

_____

_____

_____

_____

My Thoughts & Results: _____

_____

_____

_____

_____

_____

_____

_____

_____

_____

_____

_____

_____

_____

Today's Date: _____ *I'm Feeling:* _____

Frequency Exercise: _____

_____

_____

_____

_____

_____

_____

_____

_____

_____

My Thoughts & Results: _____

_____

_____

_____

_____

_____

_____

_____

_____

_____

_____

_____

_____

Today's Date: _____*I'm Feeling:* _____

Frequency Exercise: _____

_____

_____

_____

_____

_____

_____

_____

_____

_____

My Thoughts & Results: _____

_____

_____

_____

_____

_____

_____

_____

_____

_____

_____

_____

_____

_____

Today's Date: _____I'm Feeling: _____

Frequency Exercise: _____

_____

_____

_____

_____

_____

_____

_____

_____

_____

My Thoughts & Results: _____

_____

_____

_____

_____

_____

_____

_____

_____

_____

_____

_____

_____

Today's Date: _____*I'm Feeling:* _____

Frequency Exercise: _____

_____

_____

_____

_____

_____

_____

_____

_____

My Thoughts & Results: _____

_____

_____

_____

_____

_____

_____

_____

_____

_____

_____

_____

_____

_____

Today's Date: _____ *I'm Feeling:* _____

Frequency Exercise: _____

_____

_____

_____

_____

_____

_____

_____

_____

_____

My Thoughts & Results: _____

_____

_____

_____

_____

_____

_____

_____

_____

_____

_____

_____

_____

_____

_____

Today's Date: _____ *I'm Feeling:* _____

Frequency Exercise: _____

_____

_____

_____

_____

_____

_____

_____

_____

_____

My Thoughts & Results: _____

_____

_____

_____

_____

_____

_____

_____

_____

_____

_____

_____

_____

_____

_____

Today's Date: _____ *I'm Feeling:* _____

Frequency Exercise: _____

_____

_____

_____

_____

_____

_____

_____

_____

_____

My Thoughts & Results: _____

_____

_____

_____

_____

_____

_____

_____

_____

_____

_____

_____

_____

_____

Today's Date: _____*I'm Feeling:* _____

Frequency Exercise: _____

_____

_____

_____

_____

_____

_____

_____

_____

_____

My Thoughts & Results: _____

_____

_____

_____

_____

_____

_____

_____

_____

_____

_____

_____

_____

_____

_____

Today's Date: _____ *I'm Feeling:* _____

Frequency Exercise: _____

_____

_____

_____

_____

_____

_____

_____

_____

_____

My Thoughts & Results: _____

_____

_____

_____

_____

_____

_____

_____

_____

_____

_____

_____

_____

_____

Today's Date: _____ *I'm Feeling:* _____

Frequency Exercise: _____

_____

_____

_____

_____

_____

_____

_____

_____

_____

My Thoughts & Results: _____

_____

_____

_____

_____

_____

_____

_____

_____

_____

_____

_____

_____

_____

Today's Date: _____ I'm Feeling: _____

Frequency Exercise: _____

_____

_____

_____

_____

_____

_____

_____

_____

_____

_____

My Thoughts & Results: _____

_____

_____

_____

_____

_____

_____

_____

_____

_____

_____

_____

_____

_____

Today's Date: _____ I'm Feeling: _____

Frequency Exercise: _____

_____

_____

_____

_____

_____

_____

_____

_____

_____

My Thoughts & Results: _____

_____

_____

_____

_____

_____

_____

_____

_____

_____

_____

_____

_____

_____

Today's Date: _____ *I'm Feeling:* _____

Frequency Exercise: _____

_____

_____

_____

_____

_____

_____

_____

_____

_____

My Thoughts & Results: _____

_____

_____

_____

_____

_____

_____

_____

_____

_____

_____

_____

_____

Today's Date: _____ I'm Feeling: _____

Frequency Exercise: _____

_____

_____

_____

_____

_____

_____

_____

_____

My Thoughts & Results: _____

_____

_____

_____

_____

_____

_____

_____

_____

_____

_____

_____

Today's Date: _____ *I'm Feeling:* _____

Frequency Exercise: _____

_____

_____

_____

_____

_____

_____

_____

_____

_____

My Thoughts & Results: _____

_____

_____

_____

_____

_____

_____

_____

_____

_____

_____

_____

_____

Today's Date: _____ *I'm Feeling:* _____

Frequency Exercise: _____

_____

_____

_____

_____

_____

_____

_____

_____

My Thoughts & Results: _____

_____

_____

_____

_____

_____

_____

_____

_____

_____

_____

_____

_____

Today's Date: _____ *I'm Feeling:* _____

Frequency Exercise: _____

_____

_____

_____

_____

_____

_____

_____

_____

_____

My Thoughts & Results: _____

_____

_____

_____

_____

_____

_____

_____

_____

_____

_____

_____

_____

Today's Date: _____*I'm Feeling:* _____

Frequency Exercise: _____

_____

_____

_____

_____

_____

_____

_____

_____

_____

My Thoughts & Results: _____

_____

_____

_____

_____

_____

_____

_____

_____

_____

_____

_____

_____

_____

_____

Today's Date: _____*I'm Feeling:* _____

Frequency Exercise: _____

_____

_____

_____

_____

_____

_____

_____

_____

_____

My Thoughts & Results: _____

_____

_____

_____

_____

_____

_____

_____

_____

_____

_____

_____

_____

_____

Today's Date: _____I'm Feeling: _____

Frequency Exercise: _____

_____

_____

_____

_____

_____

_____

_____

_____

_____

My Thoughts & Results: _____

_____

_____

_____

_____

_____

_____

_____

_____

_____

_____

_____

_____

_____

Today's Date: _____ I'm Feeling: _____

Frequency Exercise: _____

_____

_____

_____

_____

_____

_____

_____

_____

_____

My Thoughts & Results: _____

_____

_____

_____

_____

_____

_____

_____

_____

_____

_____

_____

_____

_____

Today's Date: _____ *I'm Feeling:* _____

Frequency Exercise: _____

_____

_____

_____

_____

_____

_____

_____

_____

_____

My Thoughts & Results: _____

_____

_____

_____

_____

_____

_____

_____

_____

_____

_____

_____

_____

_____

Today's Date: _____ *I'm Feeling:* _____

Frequency Exercise: _____

_____

_____

_____

_____

_____

_____

_____

_____

_____

My Thoughts & Results: _____

_____

_____

_____

_____

_____

_____

_____

_____

_____

_____

_____

_____

_____

Today's Date: _____ *I'm Feeling:* _____

Frequency Exercise: _____

_____

_____

_____

_____

_____

_____

_____

_____

_____

My Thoughts & Results: _____

_____

_____

_____

_____

_____

_____

_____

_____

_____

_____

_____

_____

_____

Today's Date: _____ I'm Feeling: _____

Frequency Exercise: _____

_____

_____

_____

_____

_____

_____

_____

_____

_____

My Thoughts & Results: _____

_____

_____

_____

_____

_____

_____

_____

_____

_____

_____

_____

_____

_____

_____

Today's Date: _____ *I'm Feeling:* _____

Frequency Exercise: _____

_____

_____

_____

_____

_____

_____

_____

_____

_____

My Thoughts & Results: _____

_____

_____

_____

_____

_____

_____

_____

_____

_____

_____

_____

_____

_____

Today's Date: _____ *I'm Feeling:* _____

Frequency Exercise: _____

_____

_____

_____

_____

_____

_____

_____

_____

_____

My Thoughts & Results: _____

_____

_____

_____

_____

_____

_____

_____

_____

_____

_____

_____

_____

_____

Today's Date: _____ I'm Feeling: _____

Frequency Exercise: _____

_____

_____

_____

_____

_____

_____

_____

_____

_____

My Thoughts & Results: _____

_____

_____

_____

_____

_____

_____

_____

_____

_____

_____

_____

_____

_____

Today's Date: _____*I'm Feeling:* _____

Frequency Exercise: _____

_____

_____

_____

_____

_____

_____

_____

_____

_____

My Thoughts & Results: _____

_____

_____

_____

_____

_____

_____

_____

_____

_____

_____

_____

_____

_____

_____

Today's Date: _____ I'm Feeling: _____

Frequency Exercise: _____

_____

_____

_____

_____

_____

_____

_____

_____

_____

My Thoughts & Results: _____

_____

_____

_____

_____

_____

_____

_____

_____

_____

_____

_____

_____

_____

Today's Date: _____ *I'm Feeling:* _____

Frequency Exercise: _____

_____

_____

_____

_____

_____

_____

_____

_____

_____

My Thoughts & Results: _____

_____

_____

_____

_____

_____

_____

_____

_____

_____

_____

_____

_____

_____

Today's Date: _____ I'm Feeling: _____

Frequency Exercise: _____

_____

_____

_____

_____

_____

_____

_____

_____

_____

My Thoughts & Results: _____

_____

_____

_____

_____

_____

_____

_____

_____

_____

_____

_____

_____

_____

Congratulations on a successful year of raising your frequency!

☺

Live life with love, gratitude and intention to continue in forward motion along your spiritual path.

VISIT MELISSA ALVAREZ ONLINE AT
MelissaA.com, APsychicHaven.com
BookCovers.Us, .BookCoversGalore.com
Email Melissa at media@melissaa.com